GALAXY

OGHMA
CREATIVE MEDIA
Bentonville, Arkansas • Los Angeles, California
www.oghmacreative.com

Copyright © 2022 by Timothy Lange
We are a strong supporter of copyright. Copyright represents creativity, diversity, and free speech, and provides the very foundation from which culture is built. We appreciate you buying the authorized edition of this book and for complying with applicable copyright laws by not reproducing, scanning, or distributing any part of it in any form without permission. Thank you for supporting our writers and allowing us to continue publishing their books.

Library of Congress Cataloging-in-Publication Data

Names: Lange, Timothy author/illustrator
Title: Galaxy: The Best Friend a Cowboy Ever Had |
Description: First Edition | Bentonville: Lee, 2022
Identifiers: LCCN: 2022935254 | ISBN: 978-1-63373-766-2 (hardcover) |
ISBN: 978-1-63373-767-9 (paperback) | ISBN: 978-1-63373-768-6 (eBook)
BISAC: JUVENILE FICTION/Westerns | JUVENILE FICTION/Lifestyles/Farm & Ranch Life
JUVENILE FICTION/Social Themes/Friendship | JUVENILE FICTION/Animals/Horses

LC record available at: https://lccn.loc.gov/2022935254

Lee Press hardcover edition August, 2022

Cover & Interior Designer: Casey W. Cowan
Executive Editor: Chrissy Willis
Editors: Derek Hale & Amy Cowan

This book is a work of fiction. Any references to historical events, real people, or real places are used fictitiously. Other names, characters, places, and events are products of the author's imagination, and any resemblance to actual events or places or person, living or dead, is entirely coincidental.

Published by Lee Press, an imprint of Young Dragons Press, a subsidiary of The Oghma Book Group.

GALAXY

The Best Friend a Cowboy Ever Had

STORY & ILLUSTRATIONS BY

TIMOTHY LANGE

LEE PRESS

an imprint of

YOUNG DRAGONS PRESS

For Marv and Audrey

Galaxy was the best dang horse
this side of the Red River.

He was nimble as a jackrabbit,
quick as a hummingbird hiccup,

and had so much pluck, he could stare down a rattlesnake.

There was only one hitch…
Galaxy's cowboy was about as useful
as lips on a woodpecker.

His cowboy couldn't do any fancy riding.

He couldn't make a whip go "CRACK."

FLUP.

He couldn't rope.

He couldn't even spit.

Most Buckaroos had names
like Tex, or Butch, or Ringo.
Galaxy's cowboy was called Timmy.

Galaxy smoldered with embarrassment.
"You should rid yourself of that galoot,"
said the other horses.

He started to think they were right.

Yet Galaxy knew Timmy always tried his hardest.

He gave Galaxy fresh hay and water.

He brushed and curried Galaxy at the end of every day.

And he never used spurs.

But being saddled with the dullest jobs on the ranch was a problem for Galaxy.

While other buckaroos were blazing trails, Timmy and Galaxy ate dust at the back of the herd.

Instead of joining in rodeos, they scooped the poop.

When everybody else went to the shindig in town,
Timmy and Galaxy had to guard the herd.

Surrounded by dozing cows,
Galaxy felt Timmy slump in the saddle.

"Maybe he'll go to sleep and fall off," thought Galaxy. "Then I could mosey down the trail and find me a better cowboy."

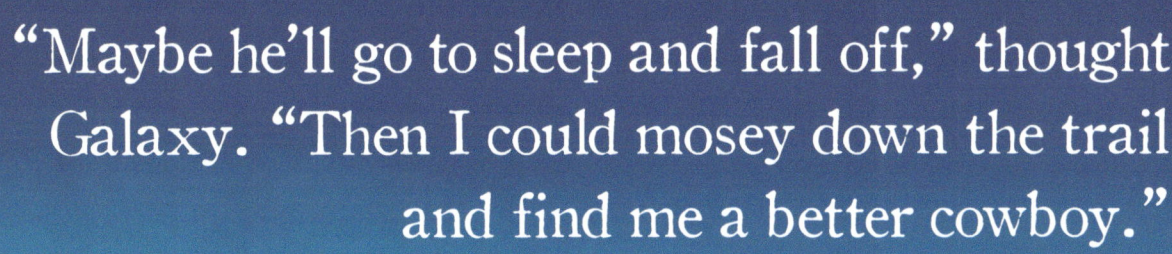

Suddenly those no-good rustlers,
the Dirt brothers, burst out of the night.

There was Red Dirt, Dusty Dirt,
and the low-down dirtiest Dirt of all, Burt Dirt.

In two shakes of a calf's tail, the herd
was in full stampede.

But when Galaxy dashed to head them off,
Timmy took a tumble.

Galaxy's chance had come.
He could skedaddle and never look back.
But Galaxy heard Timmy muttering.

"I try so hard, but I just can't get a rope around this cowboy thing. No one wants me here, and now I've lost the herd. Galaxy, I wouldn't blame you if you up and left me."

Most cowboy horses are good at running, herding, and being brave. But what kind of horse would he be if he didn't stand by his cowboy when he needed him most?

They tracked the herd to the Dirt's hideout.
"I bet those varmints are still sleeping," said Timmy.

"Here's the plan, boy."

The Dirts flew out like tumbleweeds in a tornado.

ZING

SPLAT!

Right in Burt Dirt's eye.

"Timmy got ALL them darned dirty Dirt Brothers."

"Galloping Gophers!"

"That was the BEST BIT of cowboying I EVER saw."

"DANG!"   "Boy Howdy!"

The other buckaroos reached the top of the mesa just in time to witness the whole thing.

"Galaxy, you're the best dang friend a cowboy ever had."

COWBOY GLOSSARY

Buckaroo: Another word for a cowboy.

Curried: Using a special comb just for a horse called a curry. It loosens caked mud and dirt from the horse's hair.

Galoot: A word used describe someone who is clumsy or awkward.

Herd: A large group of cattle traveling together.

Mesa: As an isolated, flat-topped elevation, ridge or hill, usually located on a plain or desert.

Mosey: Move slowly and at a leisurely pace.

Pluck: *Having spunk or courage.*

Polecat: *A weasel-like animal noted for its very, very bad smell. Also known as a skunk.*

Rodeo: *Contest where cowboys show off their skills at riding horses and bulls, roping cattle, or wrestling steers.*

Rustler: *A thief or a robber. Usually someone who steals horses or cattle.*

Saddle: *A leather seat put on a horse's back to make it easier to ride.*

Shindig: *Another word for a party.*

Skedaddle: *Get out of there in a hurry.*

Spurs: *A small spike or a spiked wheel worn on a rider's heel and used for urging a horse to go faster.*

Stampede: When a herd of animals runs away out of control.

Tumbleweed: A round scrub often found in the desert that breaks away from its roots and rolls across the plains.

Varmint: Another word for a critter or an undesirable animal.

ABOUT THE AUTHOR
TIMOTHY LANGE

Timothy Lange graduated from the Colorado Institute of Art and studied oil painting at the Art Student's League of Denver. He is a long-time SCBWI member and currently resides in Broken Arrow, Oklahoma with his wife, Penny and two goofy daughters.

Printed in the USA
CPSIA information can be obtained
at www.ICGtesting.com
LVHW071947011123
762649LV00019B/775